THE PARENT/CHILD MANUAL ON DIVORCE

THE PARENT/CHILD MANUAL ON DIVORCE

MARIA SULLIVAN

Illustrated by Chris Otsuki

TOR

THE PARENT/CHILD MANUAL ON DIVORCE

Copyright © 1988 by RGA Publishing Group, Inc.

A TOR Book
Published by Tom Doherty Associates, Inc.
49 West 24 Street
New York, NY 10010

Cover art by Chris Otsuki

ISBN: 0-812-59448-7   Can. ISBN: 0-812-59449-5

Library of Congress Catalog Card Number: 87-51394

First hardcover edition: April 1988
First tradepaper edition: July 1988

Printed in the United States of America

0 9 8 7 6 5 4 3 2 1

ACKNOWLEDGMENTS

Special thanks to Dr. Neville Kyle, clinical psychologist and Chief of Psychological Services with the Hacker Clinic in Lynwood and Los Angeles, California, for his professional advice. Dr. Kyle has specialized in children's therapy for the past twenty-three years.

Similar thanks to Michael S. Prokop, a psychologist who has worked in the Ohio school system for the past ten years. Prokop's specialization in divorce-related problems has led him to develop clinics, lecture tours, and seminars on the subject.

Thanks also to RGA Communications.

Introduction

By the end of the 1980s, an estimated 45 percent of all children in the United States will have witnessed the divorce of their parents. Each year, more than 1 million children under the age of eighteen will live through this trauma, and another 5 million will experience a significant separation of their parents. Right now, 12 million children under age eighteen have divorced parents.

Other numbers paint a picture of compounding dilemmas: 35 percent of American children in the 1980s will see at least one parent remarry, and 20 percent will endure a *second* parental divorce. Approximately 57 percent of all divorces involve couples with children.

Small wonder that children rank divorce second only to the death of a parent as a cause of anxiety. Complex feelings of anger, fear, guilt, and loneliness accompany the trauma of a family breakup, even when the split brings with it healing tranquillity.

Divorcing adults are naturally most concerned with resolving their own personal devastation—but they must also try to do everything possible to help their children through their own ordeals of loss and separation. Divorce can also be a time of communication and healing, however, and we hope that this book will aid in that process.

CHAPTER ONE

Confronting Loss

The Disruption of Personal Worlds

Divorce is now so common that we may have become desensitized to the pain it causes. All too often, we accept it as a matter of course—which underplays its effects on our lives and the lives of our children.

Let's get one issue out of the way immediately. That old rule about "staying together for the sake of the children" is often merely a thinly disguised excuse that adults use to maintain what many psychologists call *negative intimacy*. Hate can be as powerful a bond as love, and some adults lack the strength, know-how, or courage to break the destructive cycle. Better a familiar battleground than the uncertainty of change! They aren't thinking about the children at all, and they're giving their offspring the lesson that relationships are filled with anger and hostility.

The point is this: If supposedly mature adults fear going "out there" on their own, or making the adjustments that might put love back into their lives, imagine how frightened children must feel at the thought of change or an unstable future. Like their parents, they might feel it's easier to stick with what's bad but familiar than to venture out into the cold.

Take Lisa, for example. She got so used to hearing her parents argue that she learned to go into her room and put a pillow

over her head to block them out. But when she first heard her parents discussing a divorce, she panicked. Instead of realizing that at last there would be an end to the fighting, Lisa felt that she was faced with the unknown. What would happen to her and her little brother Charlie? Who would feed Sylvester, the cat? Would she still get to visit her grandparents? Putting a pillow over her head would not be enough to block out these questions.

Lisa's mom and dad can try answering her questions with a number of responses:

- "We know things are going to be different now, and we know that can feel scary. But we're all going to work together to make a lot of nice new things happen."

- "We're going to let you know exactly what will happen to you, to Charlie, and even to Sylvester! We want you to ask as many questions as you want to, about any problem, big or small."

- "I'll bet you want to know exactly how things are going to be different. We don't know all the details yet, but we'll let you know as much as we can every step of the way—and we want you to feel free to ask us anything you want."

Lisa's reaction? Relief! She won't have to figure out everything on her own, and the future seems less frightening.

Nothing in Black and White

There are many reasons why kids are so devastated by divorce. In our society, parents are a child's most powerful influence, despite the large swaying force of the media and peers. Parents act as buffers between the child and the larger world, and are responsible for meeting the child's needs. Children going through divorce often conclude that they are now unprotected.

Mark, hearing about his parents' divorce, thought that he would be abandoned. When he suggested this to his dad, he was assured that he would still be cared for:

"Just because I won't be living here anymore doesn't mean I'm not your dad, Mark. You and your mom will still live in this house, and I'm going to visit every weekend."

MARK: Who's going to take care of me?

DAD: Your mom and I are both going to take care of you, just like we do now. I won't be living here, but you can always come to me if you need something. You'll always be my son. And you can talk to me about anything that bothers you.

MARK: Anything?

DAD: Absolutely.

MARK: Well, I'd rather have you stay here. Why can't you?

DAD: It's very complicated, Mark, but your mom and I have decided that it would be better if I lived somewhere else. But you know what? I'm going to have some of those toy trucks you like at my new apartment, and a bed when you sleep over. We'll have plenty of time together.

MARK: O.K., Dad. I feel a little better now.

Not only do children owe an enormous part of their social and emotional identity to the family, there's a strong biological tie as well. The child feels connected to both parents. There's even a tinge of ownership in the child's mind; kids subconsciously feel that their parents truly belong to them.

It's not hard to understand these fierce ties, because part of the human animal's survival system is to make basic intimacies—the family bond is chief among them—as secure and solid as possible. Any rift or break in this security system will trigger a tremendous alarm.

Consider further reasons why divorce is so tough on your child. Have you ever had a son in the Boy Scouts or a daughter in the Girl Scouts? Such groups operate by a strict code of loyalty and ethics. Their rules and behaviors are spelled out clearly in black and white. Children see things as good or bad, right or wrong. Adults are better able to see the gray tones, the uncertainties and compromises, that can color the behavior that's necessary to survive in an often nonsensical world.

But children are not mini-adults. They don't always understand why bad things happen to good people. Adults can't always figure this out, either, so how can we expect our children to understand? Adults and children must all rebuild their worlds after a divorce.

Coping With Pain

As much as we'd like to spare the people we love from pain—especially our children—pain is an unavoidable part of the human experience. It comes to us all in various forms: death, betrayal, loss of love, divorce. We should not ignore it and hope it will go away, but learn how to deal with it. Part of a parent's duties is to help children develop the emotional strength that will allow them to face pain and emerge healthy and whole.

Not confronting loss or grief only prolongs these feelings and causes them to fester. That's why Mark's and Lisa's parents were right to gently urge their children to face what was happening and to encourage them to talk about their feelings.

Instead of their young imaginations running wild, Lisa and Mark might begin to see that divorce doesn't mean the end of the world. It's a real part of life. It doesn't happen only to bad kids or "bad homes." Nice kids can have divorce strike their families and still remain nice kids. Some very nice people get divorced!

Silence can be terribly destructive. Help your children express their feelings, and you'll find that when they aren't kept in the dark, they can be surprisingly open-minded and sensible.

CHAPTER TWO

The Myths
of Divorce

Finding the False Beliefs

Divorce causes an overwhelming sense of powerlessness in children. They may feel fury or despair, but often they have no idea how to express it. Their emotions stay bottled up, or explode in unpredictable ways. The reactions and needs of different children are as individual as their fingerprints.

Adults often assume from a child's silence that the child has adjusted to the divorce and accepts it. Although it's easier to understand that "bad" or aggressive behavior might be a cry for help, don't be fooled into thinking that "good" behavior signals that the child needs no guidance. All children of divorce need to express what's on their minds.

Children's minds often come alive with what Michael S. Prokop,* an Ohio psychologist and consultant who has specialized in dealing with divorce, calls *false beliefs*. When a child's fears are not addressed, and his or her sense of powerlessness feeds on itself and grows in silence, great stress and anxiety can result.

*Prokop is the author of *Divorce Happens to the Nicest Kids* and the *Kids' Divorce Workbook,* both available from Alegra Publishing, Box 1443, Warren, OH 44482. The softcover edition of *Divorce Happens to the Nicest Kids* is $10.95; the workbook is priced at $5.95. Add $1.50 per book for shipping and handling.

The child's age has some relation to how he or she will react to divorce. Very young children, aged five and under, react to divorce with sheer bewilderment. Slightly older children, ages six to nine, often feel guilty: "Mom left because my room is always a mess"; "Dad left because I broke that window"; "My parents are getting divorced because I think bad things about my younger sister." Because an adult mind wouldn't even consider these possibilities, we underestimate how distressing such feelings are for a youngster.

Anger is the most compelling drive in children aged ten to twelve. In teenagers this anger is compounded with a feeling of being cheated out of parts of childhood, of being forced to grow up too quickly.

False beliefs can take many forms:

• "I'm the cause of my parents' divorce."

• "My evil thoughts [about my brother, about wishing my father would leave] have caused the breakup."

• "If my parents divorce, I'll be abandoned and no one will take care of me."

• "If Dad leaves, then Mom will, too, and I'll be completely alone."

• "I'll never get to see my grandparents."

• "Do I have to earn money now? If I didn't ask them to buy so many things for me, would we all still live together?"

• "What will happen to my brothers and sisters?"

• "What will happen if my mom (or dad) remarries?"

• "I can't possibly be happy with only one parent."

Ask yourself if your child might be suffering from any of these false beliefs. These might become evident if you sit down with your children and address the questions that youngsters most commonly ask about divorce.

The Silent Questions

1. *"Why are you getting divorced?"* Parents don't have to "tell all." Baring your soul or disclosing every last detail, particularly regarding alcoholism, violence, or extramarital affairs, may do more harm than good. On the other hand, don't think you're "saving" your children by not telling them about a socially frowned-upon problem triggering the divorce, such as alcoholism or drug use. You don't have to go into great detail, but you should be frank with your children. What they don't hear from you, they'll hear from others. In the case of an extramarital affair, a simple "Daddy has met someone he wants to spend his time with now" might be better than ignoring a fact that could haunt your child on the playground. In short, use common sense in telling your child in a clear, concise, loving manner why you and your spouse can no longer live together.

2. *"What will happen to me because of the divorce?"* Give your child as much information as you can. If you and your spouse have not completed custody arrangements, tell your child that—and then give him or her the details as they are worked out. Explain as fully as possible what the future living arrangements will be, the monetary situation, how often he or she will see Mom and Dad, where siblings will be, and so forth.

3. *"Is this permanent?"* One of the most lingering desires of children is that the parents will reunite. You might think that the marriage was so disastrous that absolutely no one would want you and your spouse to team up again, but your children have a different view and a strong connection with both parents.

Let them know, without hostility for your spouse in your voice, that a split is permanent. Facing the truth squarely is better than giving a child false hope.

4. *"Did I do anything wrong?"* Because adults get so wrapped up in their own quarrels and sense of loss, they forget that children might feel responsible. Take the case of Jimmy, who had asked for a baseball mitt the day before his parents had a terrible fight about money. Jimmy went to talk to his dad.

"Dad?" he said. "I don't really need that baseball mitt."

"What are you talking about?" his dad asked.

Jimmy said, "I'm sorry I made you and Mom fight."

"Jimmy," said his dad, "did you think that's why we were fighting?"

Jimmy nodded and looked at his feet.

His dad said, "Listen, Jimmy, I'm sorry that your mom and I argued yesterday, but it had nothing to do with what you asked for. Money can get to be a big problem with adults, but that doesn't mean that you're responsible."

Go out of your way to explain that even though you are divorcing Mom or Dad, you will *never* "divorce" your children. If you are to be the noncustodial parent, you must take even more pains to show that absence does not mean the end of parenting. Set up definite shopping or vacation plans, show your children your new house or apartment, let them know exactly when you will be seeing them. Show them that you have beds, toys, and toothbrushes for their use whenever they come to stay.

5. *"How can divorce happen to people who were in love?"* Many children of divorce are understandably cautious when it comes to their own love relationships. It's a cliché to say, "Better to have loved and lost than never to have loved at all," but your child's emotional growth might hinge on accepting this. In discussion and by action, show your children that despite the high incidence of divorce and your own painful experience, the risk of loving is worthwhile. Ask them to recall happy times you all had together, and give examples of new happy times that lie ahead.

It won't be easy—you may feel unhappy and distrustful of love—but it's important to get on with the business of living and to give children a sense that life and belief in love will continue even in the face of trauma.

Respect your children's emotions. What a child thinks and feels does not always make sense to an adult, but that doesn't invalidate the child's worries. It's impossible to say "I love you" too often to a child. Filled with fears of abandonment, children need to hear that they are still endearing and will be taken care of. Cuddle them, play a game with them, spend some quiet time together. Give them a few islands of peace and tranquillity in the midst of upheaval.

Outline what your child's relationship will be to the non-custodial parent. One key way to get away from "broken home" imagery is to try to redefine your family in terms of restructuring: "You don't have a broken home; you have two single-parent homes!" The more the noncustodial spouse can do to continue parenting activities and contact, the more at ease children might feel.

Listen to what your child has to say, and answer his or her questions. A good rule of thumb is that a child who is old enough to think up a question is probably old enough to hear the honest answer. Don't think you're doing the child any favors by skirting issues. Here's an example of a tough situation:

LINDSAY: Dad, is it true that you're moving in with that horrible Cheryl? How could you do that to Mom?

DAD: Lindsay, I should have explained before now. I'm sorry. It's true that I will be living with Cheryl. That doesn't mean I don't still love you and your mom.

LINDSAY: Oh, come on. If you loved Mom, you wouldn't be leaving.

DAD: There are lots of different kinds of love, Lindsay, and sometimes things can get very complicated. Cheryl will never, never replace your mom. But I hope someday you will like some things about Cheryl, even though she isn't your mother.

LINDSAY: I hate Cheryl. She's fat as a pig.

DAD: I'm so sorry you've been upset by all of this,

Lindsay. I still love you very much, and you can always talk to me about whatever is bothering you.

Children are particularly afraid of a parent's new relationships. The new girlfriend, boyfriend, or spouse-to-be often bears the brunt of the child's unhappiness and fears. It's best to

let the child vent his or her feelings. You can't force a child to accept a strange person unconditionally. Lindsay's father's quiet insistence that Cheryl is a nice person but can never replace Linday's real mom is the first step toward helping his daughter adjust to her presence in his life. Best of all, because her dad did not react with anger to Lindsay's taunts about Cheryl, the girl will feel comfortable expressing even her most overpowering emotions.

Psychologists point out that some children overplay this stage of venting and adjustment. It's likely that the parent feels guilty about a new person. A child who continues to bad-mouth a spouse-to-be is setting up a potentially destructive situation. Gentle but firm discipline, plus constant reassurances of parental love, can help win the child over.

CHAPTER THREE

Creating the
Divorce Blueprint

A Time Line and Maps

According to Dr. Neville Kyle, a Los Angeles psychologist who has specialized in children's problems for twenty-three years, preparation is the key to helping your children cope with divorce. Since their anxiety is based upon their inability to predict or control the future, doing what you can to keep them informed and involved can assist your child tremendously. "To the best of your ability, create a time line and maps covering exactly what lies ahead," says Kyle.

Both parents, if possible, should sit down with the child and spell out precisely what is going to happen. Even if you're not on the best of terms, a united front is far less traumatic for the child.

Establish the boundaries of the situation. Who will keep the puppy, why Mom will have custody. When Daddy is going to move out, where he is going, how often he'll be visiting. Be honest about new people either parent might be involved with, but do not put too much emphasis on these new relationships.

Establishing and then sticking to a schedule will minimize the disruption that separation can cause. A vague "Daddy will be leaving one of these days" or "Mommy might be leaving soon" can be much more painful than saying, "On June first, Daddy will be moving into a new apartment on Ninety-eighth Street, but you'll still get to see him every weekend."

If part of the divorce settlement includes selling or moving from the family home, be particularly sensitive to your children's reactions. It's hard to be uprooted, but it can be easier if the child has a chance to see his or her new surroundings before the move. Show the child the new residence. Explain that it's still close to school, to the pizza parlor. Help him or her design his or her new bedroom.

Be as optimistic as possible about a future in which both parents will not be living under the same roof. It wouldn't hurt to explain ways in which the single-parent household will be different. The custodial parent often tries to cover all territory

formerly managed by two people, only to discover that this is impossible. Try to imagine what the day-to-day living arrangements will be for you and your children, and plan realistically.

A woman who stayed at home to raise children and is now a full-time member of the work force often feels particularly overburdened. Children would rather have a nutritious, quickly prepared meal and a more relaxed mother than a worn-down perfectionist screaming at them to enjoy an elaborate spinach soufflé.

It's possible that you and your ex-spouse will be living in somewhat reduced circumstances. That could be alarming to your children. They may feel the need to "help out." Denise and Kyle's father paid alimony and child support to their mother and was living alone in a small apartment. He made the time he spent with his children extra important. The three of them made dinner together on Fridays. Kyle and Denise took care of such small chores as buttering bread and setting the table.

That gave them a sense of helping Dad out, and they didn't have to feel guilty about his spending money on them. Remember that it's you that's important to them, not your money.

Make sure that the noncustodial parent will have as much contact as possible with the children. In many divorce cases this is the stickiest point, but the smoother the continuity in parenting by both mother and father, the less traumatic divorce is for the child. In other words, if the kids know they're still going to see Daddy, they're less likely to feel that they've lost him.

Dr. Kyle is quick to point out that these schemes are idealized to a degree. Even the most well intentioned parents can't always set aside accusations and hurt. Keep in mind that you don't have to be perfect in front of your kids. You don't always have to be calm, cool, and collected, especially when discussing your pain or other feelings. Children have a tendency to view their parents as infallible and invincible, but it won't hurt them to learn that this isn't true. Even very young children can learn that adults are only human.

Learning How to Mourn

In our rush to save our children pain, we can skim too quickly over the deep feelings produced by the long process of recovery from divorce. Separation and loss add up to grief. The death of anything that was real and important in our lives has short- and long-term repercussions. Just as they must mourn the real death of a grandparent or classmate, children must properly mourn and recover from the "death" of the family as they know it. If they don't, psychological trauma may appear years later, in adulthood.

One obstacle to mourning is the flood of peace and relief many people feel in the initial weeks or months after an unbearable situation ends. This can give the illusion of complete recovery from divorce. The child might no longer have headaches now that Daddy isn't there to get drunk after dinner and pick on everybody, and Mom might be euphoric because she met a nice man only two weeks after Daddy moved out.

If only it were that simple!

Mom's "rebound" relationship may not last, and she might be left with an increased sense of failure or loss. The child's relief will give way, as the weeks pass, to the realization that Daddy is really and truly gone.

A common pattern is that after that initial euphoria comes a depression based upon a growing recognition of loss. This is followed by denial: *This isn't really happening, there's nothing wrong, I'm completely fine.* The child may think: *Mommy will come back, this is only a bad dream.*

As time passes, grief suffuses everything. Children and ex-spouses alike become angry at abandonment. It's not too different from having a loved one die: denial gives way to grief, tinged with an often-undiscussed edge of anger that someone you loved left you.

In an emotionally healthy person, the mourning process

grows into a sense of looking ahead and getting on with life. Thoughts of the vanished loved one are not suppressed, but neither do they intrude in a destructive way on day-to-day living. Despite this, many long-range effects can still be felt. Years after divorce an adult might hesitate to form a serious relationship; a child might distrust the opposite sex.

Understanding the mourning process—relief, denial, grief, anger, and recovery—holds the key to guiding your child to as full a recovery as possible in the aftermath of divorce.

Grieving for what is lost and then recovering enough to look to the future can also help children deal with the new people in your life. Tammy felt that liking her stepfather meant she no longer loved her real dad.

"Your dad will always be special because he's your father," explained Tammy's mother, "but your stepfather loves you, too. He's a new person in our lives who wants to make life easier for both of us. How about if we give him a chance to do that?" Tammy can still grieve for the loss of her dad on a day-to-day basis, but she can also look forward to life with her stepfather.

Exercises for Children

Guiding your child through the stages of mourning may be aided by these steps recommended by Prokop:

1. Encourage even the child who appears "fine" to talk. The child may feel that "I miss Daddy" is too obvious or babyish to mention, but voicing these feelings can bring healing.

2. Don't discount how children can suffer from stress. It's true that your ten-year-old boy may not have to make executive decisions and worry about marital issues, but that doesn't mean he doesn't feel great anxieties. Encourage positive visualization, positive suggestion, and relaxation exercises for your child. Here's an example of a stress-reducer that even young children can use:

Have the child lie on his or her back, eyes closed. Starting at the feet, tighten and relax all the muscle groups of the body. Tighten and relax feet; tighten and relax ankles and calves; tighten and relax thighs, then pelvis, stomach, chest, shoulders, arms, hands—make strong fists!—neck, and finally face and scalp. Then tighten and relax the entire body. Breathe deeply throughout.

This exercise trains a child to feel the difference between tension and relaxation.

As for visualization: teach your child to lie with his or her eyes shut and picture him- or herself in pleasant surroundings:

at the beach, in a rose garden or a peaceful house. From there
it's easy to build up images of calmness. And it teaches children
to invent new dreams.

3. Remember that once is not enough in talking about divorce. Encourage children to talk about the divorce through
every stage of the mourning process, and beyond.

CHAPTER FOUR

How to Maintain "Whole House" Syndrome

The Divorce Aftermath

Let children know that there is life after divorce by adopting attitudes and using phrases that do not denote incompleteness, division, or unwholeness. A home with only one parent can be a whole house, and the breakup of a marriage doesn't mean that children are socially crippled. Here's one way of handling it:

SHELLEY: The kids at school say I'm from a broken home now that Daddy's gone.

MOM: They do? How silly! You have two homes—this one *and* your dad's.

SHELLEY: But you and Dad broke up, so why isn't this a broken home?

MOM: Because you and I have each other, and we have your dad, too, but in a different way. You're from a single-parent house, Shelley, but you still have two parents.

Avoid "now you're the man of the house" expectations. A young, bewildered boy does not need that kind of pressure. Allow him to participate in the running of the house with child-size tasks—clearing the dinner table, helping you fold laundry—but don't lay the burden of provider on his shoulders.

Divorce Maintenance

Even after your child has adjusted to the notion that Mom and Dad will no longer live together, other issues will arise.

Money problems. Money troubles are notorious for breaking up couples, and problems can extend far beyond the final decree.

If you are getting decent child support from a willing ex-spouse, you're lucky. Many women and men continue their monetary battles long after other marital hurts have subsided.

Do not under any circumstances use your children as pawns or spies. Do not manipulate them into asking Daddy for more money, and do not ask them what Mommy is up to with her new boyfriend. Ask him or her yourself.

Don't think your children are stupid, either. If your son sees you buying a huge new house, driving a new car, or taking a long vacation, telling him that you "just don't have the money" for child support simply won't wash.

You may also need to explain to your children that just because the absent parent is late with alimony or child support does not mean that he (or she) doesn't love them.

Loyalty. This is another tough issue. Never push a child into choosing between you and your ex. Although few parents actually say, "If you really love me, you wouldn't be so nice about your awful mother [or father]," many expect their children to choose sides.

Bad-mouthing your ex is doomed to backfire. If you fill the children's ears with nothing but complaints about what a terrible husband, father, provider, or lover their daddy was, they may side with you for a while. But if Daddy continues to act in a loving and generous way, they will eventually become angry with you for trying to poison them against him.

You may be completely justified in your accusations, but your children are biologically and psychologically connected to both parents and should not be asked to choose between them.

Children are not above using parents to get what they want, however. Sometimes they even threaten to leave the custodial parent and live with the other—and sometimes they make good on their threats! Allow children to express their anger with you, but do not permit yourself to be blackmailed. Children often push to see how far they can go. There is nothing wrong with insisting that they abide by the rules of the house. This will be

much easier if your ex-spouse agrees to support your decisions. A child who realizes he or she can't use one parent against the other will stop threatening to leave.

The carefree adult. Some parents go completely off the deep end after a divorce. New freedom brings with it a certain giddiness. Life turns into a young child's dream of adulthood: staying up late, coming and going as one pleases.

This is part of the euphoria stage of the mourning process. Don't confuse living your own life with having every moment be a party. Have fun—but recognize that your child's fear of abandonment may be intensified if you're rarely around.

Create homes away from home. The noncustodial parent can ease children's fears by staying as active as possible in their lives. There are practical, easy ways to achieve this participation. Children don't need lavish displays of affection and material outpourings to feel loved; they need attention and "detail work." Keep a special toothbrush, a bathrobe, games, toys, and books for them in your home. This way your children will not only feel welcome where you live, they'll feel that they belong. They're not just visitors; they're a real part of your life.

If you are the noncustodial parent, one of the best things to do is to surprise your children on "off" days. Sending cards, gifts, or other tokens of love on birthdays and holidays is fine, but it's even more exciting for children to receive special things just because you're thinking of them. No matter how busy you are, it only takes a few moments to go through your desk calendar and mark days on which to remember the kids. Mark some days "phone call," and then make the call. Even if you're out of town that day, stick to your commitment. Calling your kids while you're on the road, even for five minutes, will make them feel important.

Start a file of newspaper and magazine clippings. If your daughter loves the Seattle Seahawks, keep an eye out for articles about the team. If your son loves the guitar, save everything you find about his favorite instrument. Toss everything into a file, and mark your calendar for "mail" days. With a supply of big manila envelopes and stamps handy—buy them in a big batch, address them, affix postage right away, and then store them ready to go—it's a simple matter to pack a few items and a note and send them off. Do not underestimate the delight these remembrances can give to your faraway children.

Be prepared for outpourings of hate and anger from your child. These are natural emotions. Be understanding but don't let your child push you past your limits. Persist in loving behavior, saying, "I know you're angry, Amy, but . . ."

Many children show a certain degree of attention-getting misbehavior after a divorce. This requires your patience and understanding, but a firm "No" when necessary can be more loving than permissiveness.

Don't make the divorce the excuse for everything. Don't blame every mishap or failure on your split-up. The more easily you can move forward, the better off your children will be.

Don't expect children to repay you for your sacrifices. When your children are young, you might have to give up a certain amount of social activity. This time should be given freely, without expectations of a return. When children reach their teen years, they want to start going out with their peers, not stay at home with their parents. Let them live their own lives.

Approach your own dating and remarriage plans with discretion. Many psychologists recommend keeping new relationships fairly removed from the child, but not because you wish to hide anything. The child might become very attached to your new love interest, only to relive feelings of divorce if and when you and that person break up.

If you're the stepparent or prospective new spouse, go slowly and maintain your sense of dignity. Children will test your limits. Be patient, but don't allow yourself to be bullied. Instead of imitating what the other parent did, in hopes of winning the kids over, invent new experiences that will develop your own mutual memories. Emphasize that you are not taking the place of the missing parent and that you love the children and want to play an important part in their lives.

Children of divorce can be happy again. They haven't lost you as parents, and they should not grow up afraid to love others. They're nice kids, and they deserve all the richness that intimacy can bring.

CHAPTER FIVE

The Social Arena

The World at Large

It's O.K. if you can't meet all of your child's emotional needs during a divorce. There are many sources of help, including one-to-one counseling, teachers, and clergy. Much of our

identity depends upon how we relate to the world outside our families, and one of our survival mechanisms is to establish secondary social groups. We create safety nets, so that if we slip from the security and comforts of the primary group, we'll have other trusted people to break our fall.

You can help your children develop in a healthy, social manner by encouraging them to seek help from trusted, qualified adults. If you're a single parent trying to do everything yourself, don't be afraid to turn to child-care centers, after-school programs, and experienced baby-sitters. If you're uncertain where to go, consult the chapter of Parents Without Partners in your area. This organization has access to services and support groups that might benefit you and your children. Ask the Domestic Relations Courts for assistance. They often have guidance counseling and other services for divorced parents and their children.

It's a good idea to enlist grandparents and relatives. "Family" is an extended concept, and divorce does not mean that your child won't be Grandma and Grandpa's grandchild anymore. Your parents might be able to give the child a helpful perspective on what's happening. Other relatives can step in to act like big brothers and big sisters as well.

Teach Your Children Well

Talk with your children's teachers about how the kids are adjusting. Knowing what is going on at school can help you understand your kids. Discuss ways you and your child's teacher can help your child recover from divorce.

For young children, the teacher can encourage calming activities—painting, relaxation exercises, or reading—on Mondays and Fridays. These are usually the days in which the child is either leaving or returning to the alternative household.

Quiet times allow them to collect their thoughts. You can suggest these exercises at home as well.

Be patient about lost articles, clothing, or homework. The two-home situation easily lends itself to misplaced items.

Notice abrupt changes in a child's scholastic performance. Excessive aggressiveness or withdrawal might signal emotional trouble, and counseling might be a good idea.

Encourage children to express their feelings about divorce by giving them sentences to complete: "I wish my mother would . . ." or "What I think about my father is . . ." Sometimes all that children need is a little helpful push to talk about their feelings.

Find out about divorce groups, peer counseling, or similar activities in your area. In *Growing Up Divorced* (New York: Simon & Schuster, 1983), Linda Bird Francke writes about a six-foot orange furry creature named Orby who visits elementary schools in Warsaw, Indiana. Orby is animated by an education specialist and made to speak by a storytelling therapist from the Otis R. Bowen Center for Human Services. Through pantomimes, songs, and games, first-graders are encouraged to help Orby solve his problems with divorce. Try similar skits or exercises with your children.

Keep your children from becoming cynical about love. As they approach junior-high age, they may adopt a certain veneer of toughness that they hope will shield them from the disappointments love brings. There is no way to assure your children about love. All you can do is show them how important it is. A

kiss and a reminder to a young child that he or she is loved, or a special "I Love You!" note slipped into a lunch pail, can be a powerful reinforcement.

These are ways of showing that love can take many forms. Show your children your wedding pictures and, without bitterness, help them see how happy you were. Show them how you care for friends and neighbors, for other relatives. Be happy and loving even if there is no serious relationship on the horizon, and your children will learn that love is an emotion and state of being that does not have to depend on another person.

Perhaps the greatest lesson you can teach your children is that since they have survived the pain of loss, they are stronger, and can deal with anything the world might throw at them. Knowing that they can survive should make them willing to take risks—even to take a chance on love.

CHAPTER SIX

Read the following stories to your children to help them understand some of the fears and anxieties that divorce creates—and some of the solutions.

There are as many different responses to each situation as there are divorce cases, and it's impossible to explore all the various problems that children might confront. The situations presented here are somewhat idealized, but no less valid for that. Children and parents bring their individual needs and traits to any incident, and what works for one child or parent may not work for others. However, hearing about people from different backgrounds who are all dealing with the same dilemma might make children feel less alone.

Don't read all the stories in one sitting. You're dealing with painful emotions, and your child will need time to let everything sink in.

Use the questions at the end of the stories to encourage your child to talk about what's on his or her mind. And keep an open mind yourself, even if what the child is saying is not exactly what you want to hear.

Roberto's Story

Roberto, who was eleven, was angry. Since his father had moved to a new apartment and his mother started working in a shoe store, he was alone in the house a lot more than usual. At first it was great not to hear his parents yell at each other all the time, but soon Roberto began to feel lonely.

He wanted to have some friends over from school, but he was too embarrassed by how dirty the house was. There were dishes piled up in the sink and newspapers all over the floor. Some mornings his mother did not even make her bed. Even dinners were nothing like they used to be. When his father had lived with them, they would eat rice, tortillas, meat, and vegetables. On special occasions they would have ice cream. Now his mother served nothing but beans or frozen food.

The worse Roberto felt, the quieter he became. Finally, one of his teachers asked him what was bothering him.

"I have a terrible mother!" he blurted out. "The house is a mess and she does nothing but work and come home to

sleep!" He was shocked at how much bad feeling he'd had
bottled up inside him and wished he could take back those
hateful words.

"It's O.K., Roberto," said his teacher. "You're confused
because nothing is the same anymore. Now that your mother
works, she's doing two jobs at once. It's hard for her to be a
mother and a father to you at the same time. You know what
might make her feel better? Maybe you could help out. You
don't have to do everything, Roberto, but doing a few things
here and there will make life a little easier."

"You think so?" said Roberto.

"I'll bet if you talked to your mother about these
problems, she could help you," said the teacher. "I'm sure
she wants you to be happy."

Roberto thought about this. It sounded so simple! Why hadn't he thought about helping out? When he thought of how glad his mother would be to come home from work and find the newspapers picked up and her bed made, he raced home to do some chores. He decided that he would talk to his mother that night about some of the things that were bothering him.

Do you ever feel like Roberto did?

Kumiko's Story

At seven, Kumiko loved the playground. She liked the swings and monkey bars, and she especially enjoyed the slide. It was so much fun that she didn't mind waiting in line for her turn.

One day, when Kumiko was about to climb the slide, a bigger girl pushed her out of the way. The girl started saying mean things about Kumiko's parents getting divorced. "Your parents can't stand each other and they can't stand *you*!" she said. "Neither of them wants you anymore!"

Hearing this almost made Kumiko cry, but then she remembered what her mother had told her about the divorce: Even though they wouldn't all live together anymore, Kumiko's mother and father still loved Kumiko and her brother. The divorce wasn't her fault. It wasn't her brother's fault. Her mom and dad were still her parents.

Kumiko stood up straight and said to the girl who had pushed her, "My parents divorced each other, but they didn't divorce *me*!"

When she went home, she told her parents what had happened. They were both proud of Kumiko.

What would you say if someone said insulting things about your family?

Diego's
Story

When Diego was ten, his family moved from Chile to California to start a new life, but all their plans seemed to fall apart. His father worked two jobs; he even worked on weekends, and there still never seemed to be enough money for Diego and his parents and his two sisters and four brothers. Many nights Diego's father never bothered to come home. Finally, he left for good. Diego's mother and oldest brother both had to go to work.

Diego had trouble at home, and soon he had trouble at school as well. Some of the kids made fun of him because he didn't know much English. Before long, Diego wanted to fight anyone who crossed his path. He didn't care that the teacher was always punishing him or making him stay after school— that way, at least, he wouldn't have to go home!

One day, after Diego got into another fight, his mother took him aside. Instead of scolding him, she sat him down for a talk.

"It's rotten having Papa gone, isn't it?" she said.

"I don't care," said Diego.

"It's O.K. to be sad about it, Diego," she said. "It makes me sad."

Diego felt like crying. "I don't care," he said again, but he didn't really mean it. He felt helpless, especially knowing that his mother could be unhappy, too.

"Sometimes when we don't know what else to do, we strike out at other people," said his mama. "You know how I

yell at you and Jaime sometimes when you haven't done anything bad? I do it because I'm frustrated. It would be better for all of us to discuss what we're really mad about, instead of fighting."

Diego agreed that fighting was a waste of time. "I miss Papa all the time," he said. He knew that wouldn't bring his father back, but it made him feel much closer to his mother.

Do you ever feel angry because one of your parents has moved away?

Rachel's
Story

Rachel, who was nine, and Dorothy, two years younger, saw their father on weekends. In the year that their parents had been divorced, their father had never failed to pick them up after school on Fridays. At first it had been fun—their father would take them to soda fountains and parks. He'd let them stay up late watching TV, and on Saturday they'd go to the movies. He'd buy them popcorn and candy or insist that they go to Magic Land for the roller coaster rides. He bought them new dresses and charms for their bracelets.

Lately, though, Rachel's father had been impatient. He'd snap at them for no reason and rush them around from shop to restaurant to amusement park until they were all exhausted. Rachel and Dorothy dreaded Fridays because it meant racing around like crazy. They loved their father, but they didn't like being yelled at to hurry all the time.

"We'd better do something," said Dorothy. "Dad's getting really cranky!"

"Maybe Mom can help us," said Rachel.

Their mother was glad that the girls had come to her. "Your dad's trying very hard to show you that he loves you," she said. "How about if I mention that you'd be just as happy to go on walks with him, or to sit together and read? Maybe he's afraid that you'd be bored doing that."

"We wouldn't!" Rachel said.

"Okay, then," said her mother. "I'll tell him in a very nice way. Why don't you come up with some suggestions for what you'd like to do with your dad? That way he won't have to keep guessing."

That Friday, Rachel asked if she and Dorothy could help their dad paint his kitchen cupboards. Afterward, they could have a quiet barbecue to celebrate—and to keep out of the kitchen while the paint dried!

Rachel's father was very relieved. Instead of being a "Disneyland Daddy," he could relax with his daughters. They had a pleasant weekend together, and everybody was less hassled. The girls had realized that gifts and frantic fun weren't important—spending time with their dad was the real fun.

Do you like having quiet times with your parents?

Julius's
Story

Julius was twelve. He couldn't tell whether or not his mom and dad were going to get divorced. They lived on different sides of town, but sometimes his dad would come over and take his mom to the movies. Sometimes he would stay overnight, just like the old days.

But more and more often, Julius's parents would have a big fight and not speak to each other for days. Whenever they did this, Julius's mom made him run errands that felt like spying.

"Ride your bike over to Dad's place and pick up my sweater, O.K., sweetheart?" she'd say one day. "I left it there last week."

"Do I have to?" Julius answered. He hated doing things like this. He knew that his father would be waiting for him with angry questions about his mother. Then, when he got back home, his mother would ask about his dad. It was terrible. His two little brothers, Paul and Matt, weren't much help. "If you don't go, she'll make one of us do it," said Matt.

"Maybe you should refuse, anyway," said Paul. Paul hated to see Julius so upset. "Maybe if we all said no, this wouldn't happen."

"Last time we tried that, she wouldn't let us watch any TV. Remember?" Matt said.

"We'll think of something, Julius," Paul said. "Don't worry."

But Julius did worry. He didn't know how to say no to his mother. But he decided he had to try.

He went to talk to his mom. He said, "Mom, you know how you keep sending me over to Dad's place and asking me questions when I get home?"

"What about it?" said his mother.

"I hate being put in the middle like that, Mom."

"How are you in the middle?" she asked. She sounded really puzzled.

"You send me over there so that I can report on what Dad is doing. And he asks me what you're doing. It makes me feel awful, Mom."

Julius's mother thought about this. "You're right," she said. "I guess if I want to find something out about Dad, I should ask him myself."

Julius realized that being apart from Dad was tough on all of them—his mom, Paul, and Matt, too—and that talking about it could help them get over some of the anger. He was glad he'd told his mother how he felt.

Have you ever felt like you were caught in the middle between your parents?

Marianne's Story

"I am never going to get married!" Marianne said to her best friend, Ruth.

"I'll bet you will," said Ruth. "Why not?"

"Forget it," said Marianne, shaking her head. She had seen her parents break up, and half of her friends had divorced parents. It seemed like such terrible odds.

"Think of all the nice things you'll miss," said Ruth. "Going on trips together, building a life together with somebody, having someone there to hug, having babies and watching them grow up. I think it sounds wonderful."

"That's because your parents are still married, Ruth," said Marianne.

"No," said Ruth. "It's because I want to find someone who'll love me and whom I can love back. It seems a lot worse to me to grow up and get old and never be able to have that!"

Marianne thought about this. Even though she wasn't sure that love would last forever, being alone didn't sound like much fun. Marianne decided that sometimes love for its own sake, without guarantees, has to be its own reward. It's worth taking the chance!

What do you think?

Kevin's Story

Kevin, who was twelve, was upset. Some kids were jealous because he got very good grades. The kids would break his glasses, block his way to the drinking fountain, and call him names. They tried to pick fights with him and said ugly things about his being Vietnamese.

Kevin's father had taught him to be proud of who he was and to do the best he could, no matter what anyone said. Now that Kevin's father and mother were divorced, Kevin didn't know where to turn, or how to make these boys stop fighting with him.

"Hey, Computer Brain!" a boy yelled at him one day.
"How's it feel to be from a broken home?"

Kevin had had enough. When he got home, he told his
mother what had happened.

"It's O.K. to speak up if someone is being mean, Kevin," said his mother.

"I don't want to fight them," said Kevin.

"You don't have to," his mother said. "You can use words to make your point. You come from a single-parent home, and there's nothing wrong with that. I'll bet a lot of kids in your class do, too. Remember, your dad always told you to be proud of who you are."

The next day when a mean kid taunted him, Kevin spoke

up. "I don't come from a broken home," he said. "I come from a single-parent home, and both my mother and father take such good care of me that I don't need to go around saying terrible things to other kids!"

What would you say if someone teased you like that?

Deanna's
Story

Deanna started getting stomachaches when she first
found her mother lying drunk on the living room sofa. She
could smell the alcohol on her mother's breath. Deanna was
ten, and she didn't know what to do about her mother. She
and her brother, Tom, tried to pretend that their mother was
only sleeping, but Deanna still felt unhappy and sick.

Deanna's mother was drinking more and more. Her
father spent more and more time at the office, and Deanna
and Tom spent most of their time hiding in their rooms.

One day Deanna's father told the children that he was
leaving for good. Deanna was very upset. She knew that her
mother was sick and needed help, but that didn't seem to her

to be a good reason to break up the family. Her father should try to get help for her mother, not just leave them all. He should have come home more often.

Deanna was so angry with her parents that she couldn't speak. She wouldn't talk to Tom, and she wouldn't talk in school, even when Mrs. Simpson asked her a question. Her stomach hurt so much that she couldn't get any words out. Deanna wished she could turn into a polar bear, close her eyes, and sleep for months.

One day Deanna felt so sick that she had to go to the nurse's office. When the nurse asked her what was wrong, Deanna almost exploded. The words just came tumbling out of her. *"I'm mad!"* she shouted. *"Why is this happening to me?"*

The nurse comforted Deanna. She told Deanna that many other children had divorced parents and different kinds of problems at home, and that Deanna didn't have to feel alone anymore. Then she asked if Deanna had told her father how she felt. Deanna said she couldn't.

"Maybe if you had someone to talk to, so you could let some of your feelings out, you'd feel better. Maybe your stomachaches would stop if you didn't bottle everything up. You can tell me what's bothering you, if you want to."

Deanna sighed. Then she talked to the nurse about the

thing that bothered her the most: her mother's drinking. The nurse said she would see if she could get some counseling for Deanna's mother. She also told Deanna that whenever Deanna wanted to talk, she would listen.

Deanna was still upset, but she felt better because she had found someone she could talk to, someone who could help her family.

Is there someone outside the family who helps you when you feel upset?

Salman's
Story

Salman was seven. Sometimes his mother brought him colored pens and paper from her magazine job. She wore a nice perfume and often packed lunches for Salman and his friends to take on their Sunday morning hikes. Sometimes Salman's father sneaked him leftovers from the restaurant where he worked as a cook. On his nights off, Salman's father would tuck Salman into bed and tell him a story.

Salman loved just being with his parents. They didn't have to do or say anything special for Salman to feel good.

One day Salman's parents told him that they had become very unhappy with each other. They wanted to go

their separate ways. Salman wanted to know if it was his mother's or his father's fault that they were splitting up.

"Sometimes two people grow apart and can't get back

together," said his mom. "They do and say things to hurt
each other. But that doesn't mean that one of us is perfect
and the other is bad, Salman. Does that make sense to you?
Two good people can get divorced and still be good."

"I don't understand," Salman said. He honestly didn't
see how two people could be good and still split up.
Someone had to be right and someone had to be wrong.

"Think of your friend Joseph," said his mother.
"Remember how you used to play with him all the time? Now

you hardly ever see him—but not because one of you is bad. The two of you grew apart. You're interested in different things now."

Salman began to understand. He still liked Joseph, but they were very different, and they were not as close as they had once been. Salman knew that being married was a lot more serious and complicated than any other relationship, and that people got divorced for many reasons—but now he saw that no one person deserved the blame for a divorce. Salman hugged both of his parents and told them that he loved them both.

How did you feel when you first learned that your parents were getting divorced?

Debbie's
Story

When Debbie, who was twelve, heard that her mother was going to marry Edward, she went to her room and would not come out. She didn't want a stepfather; she wanted her real father back, not have this faker take over her life. And she didn't want to live with Edward's two sons. "I won't share my things with those awful boys!" she screamed.

Edward gave her a couple of minutes to cool off, then knocked quietly at her bedroom door. "May I come in, Debbie?" he asked.

"No!" she said. "You're not my real father, and you can't tell me what to do!"

Edward was very calm. He liked Debbie, and he understood how difficult things were for her. He talked to her

through the door. "Debbie, I'm not trying to replace your father. He'll always be your daddy. I won't take his place, but I'll be a good parent to you if you'll let me."

Ever since her parents' divorce, Debbie hadn't been sure that she trusted adults. They could promise one thing and end up doing another!

"Go away," Debbie said.

To Debbie's surprise, that's just what Edward did. Debbie expected her mother to come and argue with her, but

instead everybody left her alone. She did a lot of thinking, but she still felt angry.

The next day at school, Debbie was sitting alone on the playground. A girl named Gloria came over to talk to her. Gloria was very popular and seemed happy with life. Debbie thought that Gloria could never understand her problems, and she didn't know what Gloria wanted.

"You look like what I looked like after my parents broke up," said Gloria, who had heard about the divorce through the grapevine.

"Your parents are divorced?" Debbie said. She couldn't believe her ears.

"Sure. And my dad's remarried. I have five stepbrothers! What a mess!" Gloria laughed, as if it didn't bother her at all.

"Don't you hate it?" said Debbie. "I hate them all. My mother's going to marry this awful creep." As soon as the words left her mouth, Debbie felt silly. Edward wasn't really a creep, and she knew that her mom was very fond of him. She hesitated, then said, "Edward's not all that bad. I just don't want him around all the time."

"I know the feeling," Gloria said, sitting down next to Debbie. "I was so mad that I practically didn't talk to my stepmom for a year!"

"Really?" asked Debbie.

"Sure," said Gloria. "It takes a long time to get used to having a new parent, but you will. I did. I even got used to having five brothers! Give the guy a chance."

"O.K.," Debbie said. It was a big comfort to know that someone who had gone through the same thing could seem so content. Debbie figured it would take a while to adjust to Edward, but if Gloria could get used to a stepmom—and five new brothers—she could get used to having a stepdad—and only two brothers. Maybe she could even help with the wedding.

"Come on," Gloria said. "Let's go play volleyball!" The two girls ran across the playground to join the game.

How would you feel if one of your parents wanted to get married again?

Paul's
Story

After Paul's mother and father were divorced, his dad moved far away to Montana. When Paul was eight, he went to live with his father for the summer. Paul was excited by the thought of learning how to ride horses and raise cattle. His father had promised him cookouts and camping trips. Paul was going to be a real, live cowboy!

But it didn't work out. Two weeks after Paul arrived in Montana, his dad started to ignore him. Paul didn't know why. He tried to do everything right, but his father still acted disgusted with him. They didn't do any of the fun things his

father had promised. Then one afternoon Paul's dad said, "Having you come here was a bad idea. I think you'd better go home tomorrow."

Paul had no idea what he'd done to make his father so mad. He had never felt worse in his life. He started crying and couldn't stop.

When Paul got home, his mother tried to comfort him. "Your father isn't really mad at you," she said. "He might still be mad at me because of our divorce. You probably reminded him of me. Or maybe he realized that he couldn't take care of you the way he wanted. It's hard to know for sure. Sometimes adults don't know how to express their feelings."

Once Paul realized that it wasn't his fault, he felt a little better. He hoped that one day he and his dad would be able to spend time together, but in the meantime they could call each other or write letters. They would have their own lives.

Have you ever been disappointed when you visited the parent you don't live with?

Harvey's
Story

Harvey, who was nine, thought that there were some
nice things about living with his dad after the divorce, like
going to baseball games and fishing in the lake. But
sometimes he felt rotten inside and sometimes he missed his
mom.

Harvey's father had begun dating a woman named
Joyce. Joyce tried to be friendly with Harvey and his younger
brother, Andrew. Once she bought them a new soccer ball.
Harvey sort of liked Joyce, but when she and his father
kissed and hugged right in front of them, Harvey felt sick. At
night Harvey would put a pillow over his head to block out the

laughter he could hear from his father's bedroom. Sometimes Andrew did the same thing.

Harvey tried to talk to Andrew about how he felt, but Andrew pretended that there was nothing wrong. "I don't know what you're talking about. I like Joyce," said Andrew, who was six.

"Doesn't it bother you when they kiss in front of us?" Harvey asked.

Andrew just shrugged, but Harvey could tell that Andrew was just as uncomfortable as he was. He decided that since he was older, he would have to talk to their dad.

One morning at breakfast, Harvey took a deep breath

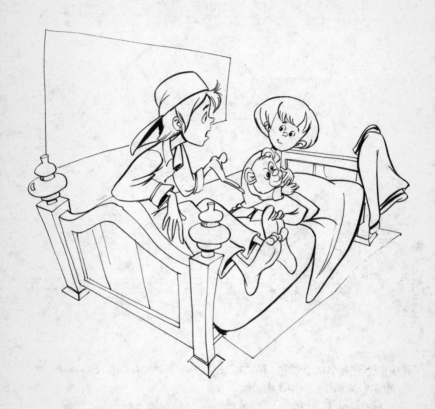

and said, "Dad, I like Joyce very much, but sometimes when the two of you are together, I hear and see things that make me very uncomfortable."

Harvey's father hadn't realized that he'd been making his son unhappy. "Harvey, I'm sorry," said his father. "I didn't know that it bothers you when Joyce and I are affectionate. I hope it will bother you less as you get to know her. She's not trying to replace your mother, if that's what's worrying you." Harvey's dad put one arm around Harvey and one around Andrew. "I'm really glad that you could talk to me about your feelings. Joyce and I will try not to kiss in front of you for a while, O.K.? Maybe that will help."

"Maybe it will, Dad," Harvey said. He felt much better now that he'd talked to his dad. His feelings didn't have to be a secret anymore.

How would you feel if one of your parents had a new boyfriend or girlfriend?

Concepción's
Story

Concepción was ten, and her parents had been divorced for a few months. She saw her dad once a week, and he was always nice to her. Sometimes he, his new girlfriend, Teresa, and Concepción would go to the zoo. Teresa had a pretty laugh. Once she bought Concepción barrettes for her hair. At first Concepción hadn't liked her, but it was hard to stay mad or silent around someone who was trying to be kind.

Concepción's problem was going back to her mom afterward. The second Concepción walked in the door from seeing her dad, her mother would start asking what Teresa did or said. Concepción loved her mother, but she didn't like answering a hundred questions about Teresa.

"I don't know," Concepción would say, hoping her mother would stop asking questions if she didn't get answers. This never worked. Her mother was still so angry about Concepción's father that she said horrible things about him, no matter what Concepción said.

Concepción felt that if she liked Teresa, her mother would be upset. And she was mad because her mom would only use awful words about her dad. Everything was all mixed up! Concepción knew that something had to be done.

Finally, she said to her mother, "Mom, I don't see Dad very much anymore, and I want to enjoy my time with him. Please don't ask me to spy on him. It makes me very uncomfortable."

"I'm not asking you to spy!" said her mother. She sounded shocked.

"That's what it feels like," Concepción insisted.

"Maybe you're right," said her mother, thinking about

how she had been acting. "I didn't realize that's what I was doing."

"I love you both," said Concepción. "I don't want to have to choose between you. And I think Dad will tell you whatever you want to know, if you'd just ask him."

What would you say if you were in Concepción's place?

Pat's Story

According to his parents, who were always yelling at each other, everything at Pat's home was a mess. Pat's father complained about the house, and his mother would say, "The house is falling apart because our bank account is such a mess, and that's your fault!"

Pat, who was eight, looked around his bedroom and thought that he was to blame for these terrible fights. There was laundry piled up on his floor, baseball cards everywhere, and dust on the windowsills. There was even an old doughnut box under the bed. No wonder his parents were talking about getting a divorce!

Pat cleaned up his room. He vacuumed the rug, dusted the furniture, and picked up his T-shirts. He fed the dog. He washed the breakfast dishes and made sure that everything was in order before he left for school in the morning. It was a lot of work, but it seemed a small price to pay for keeping his parents together.

Pat got a terrible shock the afternoon his father sat down with him and said, "Your mother and I have decided that we can't live together anymore."

"I'll keep my room clean!" said Pat. "I promise I'll be good!"

"Pat," said his dad, "you already are good. You're a wonderful son, and we know this has been a painful time for you. You must understand that you are not the cause of what has happened."

It took a while for this to sink in, but eventually Pat began to see that keeping two people's lives neat and tidy is not

nearly as easy as keeping a room clean and orderly. He was sad about his parents' divorce, but he decided that it was not happening because he'd been bad.

Do you ever think that you are the cause of your parents' divorce?

Christine's Story

Christine could not believe the awful news. Not only were her parents getting a divorce, but they planned to sell the house! She wouldn't have the same old closet and that pretty lemon tree outside her window. She sat on her bed hugging her stuffed bear, not knowing what to do.

Her mother walked into Christine's room and sat on the edge of the bed. "Chrissy," she said, "talk to me. I hate to see you so unhappy."

Christine knew her mother was trying to help. "Don't sell the house, Mommy!" she blurted out. "I don't want to leave here!"

Christine's mother gave her a big hug and a kiss. "This is all very confusing for you, isn't it? Let me try to explain.

Tomorrow, after school, I'm going to take you to see the new place where you and your brother Benjamin and I are going to live. I'll show you your new room. It's bright and sunny, and you know what? There's a big, beautiful rosebush right outside your window!"

"But I want to stay here." Christine was six; she'd never lived anywhere else.

"I know what you mean," said her mom. "I wish we didn't have to sell this house, either. But we have to, because Daddy and I need the money. I know where all my books and pots and pans are here, and I'll need time to get used to a

new place just like you will. We're going to have to help each other out, Chrissy."

"What about Daddy?"

"He doesn't want you to feel bad, either. You'll have a room there, too, and a little desk set up just for you. And your teddy bear can go along when you visit."

Since her mother explained some things, Christine began to feel better. Maybe she would like the new house, after all.

How would you feel if you had to move?

Samantha's Story

Samantha was furious with her mother for bossing her around. Samantha, who was eleven, was older than Lucy, who was still a baby, and Sean, who was seven, but it wasn't fair that she had to do so many chores. The list seemed endless: running to the store for baby food, doing the dinner dishes, taking out the trash, finishing her homework. Weekends with her dad were a lot more fun—and less busy!

One day, when her mother told her that she couldn't go out and play until she'd cleaned her room and helped Sean with his homework, Samantha got really angry. "No!" she yelled. "I'm tired of doing all the work around here! I hate living here! If you don't leave me alone, I'll go live with Dad!"

Samantha stormed into her room. She had to get out of that crazy house! The more she thought about it, the more

living with her dad seemed like a good idea. He let her do whatever she wanted and he loved her. Samantha decided she belonged with him.

The next day, after school, Samantha took a bus to her dad's house. She waited outside until he got home from work. "Dad!" she shouted, giving him a hug. "I'm going to live with you now. Mom's always being mean to me."

Samantha's father was very surprised to see her, and more surprised to hear what she had to say. He sat next to her on the porch. "Does Mom know that you're here right now?"

"No," Samantha said. "She doesn't care, anyway."

"I'll bet she's very worried because you haven't come home from school."

This was not what Samantha wanted to hear. Why wasn't her dad excited about having her live with him? Maybe he didn't understand. "Dad, I want to live with you all the time," she said. "Mom is always making me work!"

"Sam," said her father, giving her a hug, "you know how much I love you. I wish we could be together all the time. But you belong with your mother and your brother and sister. Living here wouldn't be any easier than living there. There and here are the same. No TV until your homework is done. Bedtime at ten o'clock. Baths every night. You'd have to help with the cooking and cleaning, and you'd have to have a baby-sitter every afternoon while I'm at work."

Samantha thought that life with her father wouldn't be any easier, after all—and she'd miss Sean and Lucy. But her mom would be mad because she ran away.

"I can't go back now," she said.

"Sure you can," her dad said. "I'll call Mom to let her know that you're O.K. and see if you can stay for dinner. We both know how upsetting this divorce is for you, and I don't think you'll be punished for running away."

"I promise I won't run away again," Samantha said. She felt a little better.

Her dad got to his feet and helped Samantha up. "That's my girl," he said. "You know, Mom might not realize that she's asking you to do too much. Why don't you talk to her about it?"

"I will," Samantha said. Now that she saw how easy it was to talk to her dad, maybe talking to her mom wouldn't be so tough!

Have you ever been so upset that you wanted to run away?

Jason's Story

Jason liked doing things with his mother. Since he was an only child and his parents were divorced, his mom didn't have anyone else. Jason took her to his softball games and stayed around the house on weekends so she wouldn't have to be alone. He went shopping with her and helped her with the herb garden.

He spent a lot of time with his dad, too. His father liked his company and often asked him to come over and watch sports on TV with him. Jason, who was eleven, sometimes felt a little bit sorry for his dad, who lived in a tiny, dark apartment and didn't seem to have many friends. Lots of times Dad would just drive out and get Jason, even though he lived in a different city.

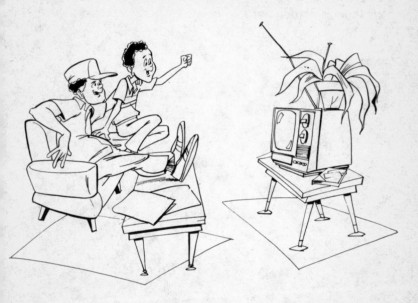

One Saturday Jason's friends wanted him to come to the movies. Mrs. Chung, the mother of one of the boys, planned to pick them all up and take them out for hamburgers afterward. It sounded like fun, but Jason had a problem. He knew that his mother wanted him to help her clean out the attic. He also knew that his father wanted him to come over and watch the football game.

Jason felt very torn up inside. He felt guilty about wishing that his parents would find things to do without him. But he wanted to be with his friends.

"Mom, can we clean out the attic next week?" he asked. "I'd like to go to the movies. Mrs. Chung will drive me there and back." He felt sad about leaving his mother alone, but he knew that he had to live his own life sometimes, too.

"I think that's a great idea," said his mother. "Mrs. Chung is very nice to drive you. Maybe sometime I can take you and your friends somewhere."

Jason decided to have the same talk with his dad. He called his father and said, "Dad, I know how much you like watching football with me. I like it, too. But I have a chance to go to the movies with my friends. Can we watch a game together some other time?"

Jason's father said that was O.K. with him. "It's good for you to get out with your friends," he said. "Maybe you can tell me all about the movie." Jason's dad also said that some weekend he'd take Jason and his pals to a real football game. Jason was pleased to see that not only could he go off on his own, he could include his friends in his parents' lives.

Have you ever had Jason's problem?

Marla's
Story

Marla had always been a happy girl. She had a good friend named Amelia who loved to sleep over at her house on weekends. They would paint their fingernails and whisper about boys, but they would also go to each other when they were upset or confused about something. That's what friends are for.

Marla's life was pleasant in many other ways. She was doing well in fifth grade. She played the flute, and one day she hoped to play in an orchestra. She had many wonderful plans for her future.

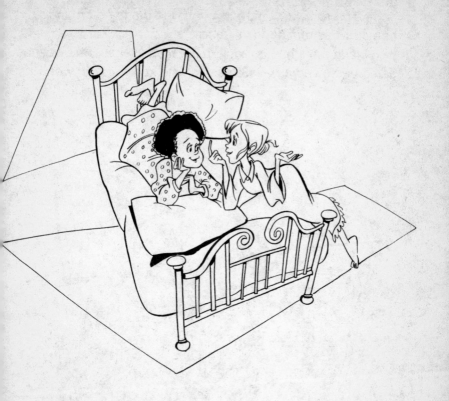

Those dreams seemed to shatter the day Marla
discovered that her parents were getting a divorce. That was
bad enough, but her father had been secretly dating another
woman and had gone to live with her. She couldn't believe it.
Her parents had always been so quiet. They had hardly ever
raised their voices. How could this be happening?

Marla turned to Amelia for comfort and got another
shock. Amelia didn't want to talk to her. In fact, she acted as
if she didn't want to be Marla's friend anymore.

"What's wrong?" Marla asked.

"Only bad families get divorced," said Amelia. "Only bad

homes break up. My parents only want me to be around people who are a good influence."

Marla thought this didn't make much sense. She was the same person as always. Besides, she knew of plenty of

decent families that had been through a divorce.

She was so upset by what Amelia said that she went straight to her mother. "Amelia says that we're a bad home now!"

"Do you think that's true?" her mom said.

Marla thought a moment. "No," she said. "I haven't done anything wrong."

"That's right, Marla," said her mother. "Do you think it would help Amelia to understand if I called her mom and we talked about this?"

"Maybe," Marla said.

"Okay, then," said her mother. She dialed Amelia's mom right away. The two mothers talked for a while, and then Marla was handed the phone. Amelia was on the line.

"Hi, Marla," Amelia said. "You know what my mom just told me? 'Sometimes divorce happens to the nicest kids!' Please forgive me. I can't stand not being your friend!"

"Neither can I," said Marla. And both girls laughed.

What would you think if one of your friends acted like Amelia?

Derek's Story

Derek got a paper route after school because he couldn't stand going home. He would stretch out the time as long as he could, but after delivering the papers he could do nothing except return to the nightmare. His father was out of work and drank whiskey and beer all day and all night. He beat up Derek's mother. He would grab her by the hair and throw her against a wall or punch her in the stomach. If she yelled that she was going to leave him, he only hit her harder.

At first Derek tried to protect his mother, but he was only nine and his father was much bigger. He would beat Derek, too.

Derek didn't understand what his mother was doing wrong. As far as Derek could tell, his mom was trying to make their lives better. She was taking a night class at a local

high school, learning how to be a travel agent, and she was very careful to save money.

Derek was afraid to tell anyone what was happening at home. He was sure that if he did, his mother would abandon them. As much as he hated what was happening to her, he was more afraid of losing her.

But Derek felt so horrible about his home that one day at

school he broke down and told Mr. Gonzalez, his teacher, the truth.

"You're brave to step forward, Derek," said Mr. Gonzalez. "Your mother needs help, and so does your father. What he is doing should not be kept a secret. If your parents

get a divorce, it will be because they cannot live together without these terrible things happening, not because you told me the truth. First we are going to put your mother and you and your brother and sister in a place where you will be safe, and then we'll get some help for your dad."

Mr. Gonzalez gave Derek's shoulder a reassuring squeeze. Derek felt good about telling him about the troubles at home, even if it meant his parents might get a divorce.

What would you do if you were Derek?

Lisa's
Story

Dinnertimes were hard around Lisa's house. Either her mother and father yelled and called each other names, or they were so silent that every noise Lisa and her brother and sister made seemed to echo. Lisa hated how often her mom and dad used the word "divorce." Thinking about it made her head hurt.

One day Lisa felt so sick that she stayed in bed. She liked first grade, but she just couldn't get up for school. When her mother asked what was wrong, Lisa said, "You're going to divorce me, too, aren't you?" and she started to cry.

"No, that will never happen," said her mother. "Even if I don't stay married to your father, I won't stop being your mother. You'll always be my little girl, no matter what happens."

"What about Tina and Bob?" Lisa was worried that she would be separated from her sister and brother.

"They're going to stay right here with you," said her mother. "Lisa, we will tell you all of our plans as we make them. Is there anything else you want to talk about now?"

"I don't want Daddy to move out," Lisa said.

"I know that's horrible to think about," her mother said. "But he'll still be your daddy. We'll show you where he will live and tell you when he will come to see you, Tina, and Bob."

"I don't like it," said Lisa. She'd stopped crying.

"It isn't easy for any of us," her mother agreed. "But doesn't it feel a little better to talk about it?"

Lisa nodded. She knew things wouldn't be perfect, but she learned that it was better to speak up than to keep her secret fears locked inside.

Does divorce frighten you?

Phillip's Story

Phillip was furious at his father. His dad had promised he'd call on Phillip's ninth birthday, and here it was two days later . . . and still no phone call!

"He's late with the check to Mom this month, too, Phil," said his teenaged sister, Miriam. "Can you believe it?"

Phillip tried to remember if his dad had been like that when they were living together as a family. His mother had always said that their dad was "married to his work." Phillip wasn't sure what that meant, except that his dad never seemed to be around very much.

"I hate him," Phillip told his mother. "I don't care if you punish me for saying that. Miriam hates him, too."

"You bet," Miriam yelled from the kitchen. "If he actually remembered my birthday on time, I'd fall over in a dead faint!"

"I don't blame you for being upset," said their mom. "I used to get mad at him for being late about everything, but one day I realized that it didn't mean he didn't love us."

"He sure has a funny way of showing it," Miriam yelled. "Give me a break!"

"Miriam, instead of hollering, why don't you come into the living room and talk with Phillip and me?"

Miriam appeared with a dish towel in her hand. "You

don't have to defend Dad all the time, Mom," she said.

"Think about it, though," said their mother. "He never completely forgets about us, he's just late. Believe me, I'd much rather have him be on time, but I also know that probably tomorrow he will call you, Phillip. And the check will arrive by the end of the week, same as always."

"He can't be that busy," said Phillip.

"Being late is the way your dad is," said his mother. "Sometimes when we love people, we have to overlook their worst habits. That doesn't mean that we like those habits or that they don't upset us, but we have to see beyond them, to what the person is really like. Don't you want to think that Dad is doing the best he can, or would you rather stay mad at him?"

"I want him to do better," said Phillip. "What's so hard about writing out a check for you or remembering my birthday?"

"Have either of you ever thought to tell your father what you've told me?" said their mother.

"He wouldn't listen," said Miriam.

"How do you know until you've tried?" said their mother.

"If he's always been this way, how is saying something going to change him?" said Phillip.

"Maybe it won't," said their mother, "but at least then you'll know that you told him what was on your mind. That's better than letting your anger build up."

Phillip saw that his mom was right. If all this lateness bothered him, he should bring it up with his dad.

What would you do if you were Phillip?

Ginger's
Story

Ginger was almost in tears. She'd had a very tough day at school. She'd forgotten her homework at her dad's house, where she'd spent the weekend. Mrs. Dexter, her third-grade teacher, had scolded her in front of the whole class.

It got so confusing sometimes, trying to remember what she kept at her mom's house, and what she left at her dad's. Only last week she'd left her raincoat behind when Shana, her dad's new girlfriend, had come to pick her up for the weekend. Her little brother, Teddy, had forgotten his raincoat, too.

Shana had been angry with Ginger and Teddy. "You have to stop being so careless, Ginger!" Shana had said that day in the car. "I don't have time to go all the way back to your mother's house. Your father wanted to take you to the lake tomorrow—and you can't go without your raincoat. You've ruined his nice plans!"

Ginger had kept quiet. She didn't like being lectured by Shana. Shana was always in such a big rush, and she was way too bossy. She made Ginger nervous. Teddy stared at his feet whenever Shana yelled at them. What was the big deal about raincoats? Why couldn't they go to the lake with an umbrella or buy a couple of those cheap rain ponchos at the drugstore?

That day, when Ginger got home from school, her mom noticed that she looked unhappy. "How about if you get out your Magicland game, Ginger? Let's play a round before you do your homework."

That sounded like a good idea to Ginger. She went to the closet where she and Teddy kept their toys and looked through the pile of board games. Magicland wasn't there. Then she remembered that she'd taken it to her dad's house two weekends ago. For the second time that day, tears of frustration welled in her eyes. Everything in the world was out of place!

"Ginger," said her mom, "you look as if you're about to burst into tears. What's wrong?"

"Nothing," said Ginger, and began to cry. She knew how tough the divorce was on her mom, and she didn't want to complain about her silly little problem.

"Are you sure, sweetheart?" said her mother. "I'll bet something is bothering you. Is it about Dad? Is something wrong at school?"

"I'm always getting yelled at," she said, "and I hate it."

Ginger's mom put her arms around her. "Tell me who is yelling at you, and why," she said.

"It's not important," said Ginger.

"It *is* important," said her mom. "If something is bothering you this much, I want to know about it."

"It's just that I can never remember where anything is!" said Ginger. She felt as if she were about to explode with anger. "Magicland is at Dad's house! Shana got mad at us last week for forgetting our stupid raincoats! I'm always leaving my homework one place or another, and today Mrs. Dexter scolded me. It was terrible!"

"I'm sure it's frustrating for you and for Teddy," said her

mom. "Sometimes we adults get so wrapped up in our own problems that we forget what is happening to you. Have you thought of talking to your dad about this? Maybe he and Shana and I can work something out. Maybe we can be extra careful to keep track of what you bring over to their house on the weekend and make sure you have everything when you come back on Sunday night."

"Shana is too bossy. I can't talk to her," said Ginger.

"Shana has a tough job, Ginger," said her mom. "She's not your mother, but she has to act like it for a few days a week. She doesn't have time to relax. She probably wants everything perfect, and maybe that makes her impatient."

"I can't complain about her to Dad," said Ginger.

"You don't need to complain," said her mom. "I'll talk to him, and instead of blaming anybody, I'll suggest that the adults all help you and Teddy take care of your homework, clothing, and toys when you go there for weekends. But you should talk to Dad when things like this are bothering you. He wants you to be happy, and so does Shana."

"Okay," said Ginger.

"And if Mrs. Dexter scolds you again, let Dad or me know. Maybe we can explain to her how tough this going back and forth is for you, and she'll be more understanding in class."

Ginger couldn't believe how relieved she felt already. "Thanks, Mom," she said. "You're the greatest!"

What would you do and say?